From the Belly

of My

Beauty

Volume 38

Sun Tracks
An American Indian Literary Series

Series Editor
Ofelia Zepeda

Editorial Committee
Vine Deloria, Jr.
Larry Evers
Joy Harjo
N. Scott Momaday
Emory Sekaquaptewa
Leslie Marmon Silko

From the Belly of My Beauty

Poems by
ESTHER G. BELIN

THE UNIVERSITY OF ARIZONA PRESS   TUCSON

The University of Arizona Press
© 1999 The Arizona Board of Regents
All rights reserved

∞This book is printed on acid-free, archival-quality paper.
Manufactured in the United States of America

10 09 08 07 06 05   7 6 5 4 3 2

Library of Congress Cataloging-in-Publication Data
Belin, Esther G.
From the belly of my beauty: poems / by Esther G. Belin.
p. cm. — (Sun tracks; v. 38)
ISBN-13: 978-0-8165-1954-5 (alk. paper)—
ISBN-10: 0-8165-1954-4
1. Indian women—California—Los Angeles Poetry.
2. Navajo Indians Poetry   I. Title.   II. Series.
PS501.S85 vol. 38 PS3552.E   99-6335
810.8'0054 s—dc21
[811'.54]

Publication of this book is made possible in part by the proceeds of
a permanent endowment created with the assistance of a Challenge
Grant from the National Endowment for the Humanities, a federal
agency.

Monotype illustration on cover and woodcut illustration in text,
© Esther G. Belin

The manifestation of this book
comes from the love and
strength of our creator. I am
thankful for my acquaintance
with Ruthie and Sierra Edd,
Jon Davis, Arthur Sze and
Simon Ortiz.
My path on
this earth is
paved well.
This book
grows from
and is a con-
tribution to
human existence on this planet.
Nízhóní like that.

CONTENTS

I.

Blues-ing on the Brown Vibe 3

He Changed the Whirl in My Palm 7

Directional Memory 8

Jenny Holzer Inspiration 10

On Relocation 11

Check One 12

Bringing Hannah Home 13

March 11, 1995 15

Ruthie Rae, My Kid 16

Case Study #311,990 17

Indian Mom 19

Euro-American Womanhood Ceremony 20

Asdz'aan Tó'dichi'níí 21

II.

Ruby Awakens 25

Ruby's Summer Fruit 27

Ruby Roast 28

Ruby in the Sky 29

How Ruby Saves Laughter 30

Disco Danny AKA Ruby's Dance Partner 32

Ruby at Bat 33

Ruby Stew 34

How Art Opens Ruby's Eye 35

Ruby's Bird Cage   36

Ruby Hikes   37

Ruby in Me #1   39

Ruby in Me #2   40

Ruby's Answer   41

Ruby's Welfare   43

Ruby and Child   45

Falling Stars   46

III.

Dry Spell   49

To Imagine Her Whole, Once More   50

949 Agua Fria   51

Sending the Letter Never Sent   52

For Miss Celine When She Smokes   54

Night Travel   56

2 + 2 = Too Much   58

"49" in a Mountain Town   60

On *Telly Biliizh*   61

When Roots Are Exposed   62

To the Word "Indian"   64

IV.

In the Cycle of the Whirl   67

I.

The beckon for liberation itches on my
back. I scratch desert-dried arroyos littered
with fading Budweiser cans and roadside
crosses dangling plastic flowers. I stumble
from the grotesque reflection recycled. I
stumble with my commod-filled body
running a Wheaties race. I stumble at my
shadow raised by Los Angeles skyscrapers.

My expression is a liberation functioning as
a contrived reality boxed into *Indian*.
Identifying the branches of soul wounds
into another contrived reality called
American AKA United States. In power
until we salt our tongues bridging callused
shoulders. A great wall of burnt flesh.
Ideographs. Tongue swollen from word
arrows. Our stories etched on our backs.
Reading our backs does not start the
healing process. To be cleansed with winds
from Canyon de Chelly. Luster of precious
stones hundreds of years smooth.

Blues-ing on the Brown Vibe

I.
And Coyote struts down East 14th
feeling good
looking good
feeling the brown
melting into the brown that loiters
rapping with the brown in front of the Native American Health
    Center
talking that talk
of relocation from tribal nation
of recent immigration to the place some call the United States
home to many dislocated funky brown

ironic immigration

more accurate tribal nation to tribal nation

and Coyote sprinkles corn pollen in the four directions
to thank the tribal people
        indigenous to what some call the state of California
        the city of Oakland
for allowing use of their land.

II.
And Coyote travels by Greyhound from Albuquerque, New Mexico,
    USA thru
Dinétah
to Oakland, California, USA
laughing
Interstate 40 is cluttered with RVs from as far away as Maine

traveling and traveling
to perpetuate the myth
Coyote kicks back for most of the ride
amused by the constant herd of tourists
amazed by the mythic Indian they create

at a pit stop in Winslow
Coyote trades a worn beaded cigarette lighter for roasted corn
from a middle-aged Navajo woman squatting
in front of a store

and Coyote squats alongside the woman
talking that talk
of bordertown blues
of reservation discrimination

blues-ing on the brown vibe
a bilagáana snaps a photo
the Navajo woman stands
holding out her hand
requesting some of her soul back
instead
she replaces her soul with a worn picture of George Washington on a
    dollar bill

and Coyote starts on another ear of corn
climbing onto the Greyhound
the woman
still squatting
waiting
tired of learning not to want
waits there for the return of all her pieces.

III.
And Coyote wanders
right into a Ponca sitting at the Fruitvale Bart station
next to the Ponca is a Seminole
Coyote struts up to the two
"Where ya' all from?"

the Ponca replies
"Oooklahooma"
pause
the Seminole silent watches a rush of people climb in and out of the
    train
headed for Fremont
the Seminole stretches his arms up and back stiff from the wooden
    benches
pause
he pushes his lips out toward the Ponca slowly gesturing that he too
    is from Oklahoma
Coyote wanders
"Where 'bouts?"

the Ponca replies
"Ponnca City"
pause
the Seminole replies
"Seminoole"

Coyote gestures to the Ponca
"You Ponca?"
the Ponca nods his head in affirmation
Coyote nods his head in content

to the Seminole
Coyote asks
"You Seminole?"
pause
the Seminole now watching some kids eating frozen fruit bars
nods his head

and Coyote shares his smokes with the two
and ten minutes later
they travel together on the Richmond train
headed for Wednesday night dinner at the Intertribal Friendship
   House.

IV.
And Coyote blues-ing on the urban brown funk vibe
wanders
in and out of existence
tasting the brown
rusty at times
worn bitter from relocation.

He Changed the Whirl in My Palm

Hands chiseled from earthen clay
show me
how to see
a bird on a face
24-year flight
lost child
finding home.

Directional Memory

West

Let's begin with the first thing you remember.
You lost a sandal in the move from the apartment on Mulford to the
house on Poplar Drive.
Specific memory of wanting to go back and get the shoe and in your
head you even telepathically announce to everyone that you left your
shoe at the old home. Never to be seen again. Part of you left behind.
Never to be seen again.

North

Kissing me with your red lips
blessing me with your diva-ness
shiny black hair dances at Mr. Fives
swinging wet with heat
steam from the jungle you emerged
traces my image in blues ultra.
Our touch moved people off the dance floor and out of recliners.
Our touch tack-sharp tickled memories
of Maxine Hong Kingston and Norman Mailer and Gary Snyder
    trying to levitate
the Pentagon
of small children selling Chiclets
trying to levitate their image to heaven.
Our touch tender as ginger on tongue forks into the two of us.

South

Christmas night in Southern California

rollerblading on the strand

night fishing off Hermosa Pier.

Walking on the beach wanting to sleep there

not wanting to awaken in someone's private property, saying it's a
    drag

waiting to get a piece, saying it's a drag

'cause that sand belongs to the six-million-dollar home in the back-
    ground.

When you were little the water called your name to jump in

same as the stench of contamination warns you to stay out

If all the sand in my boots could build my castle . . .

East

When the awe of downtown Los Angeles scratches my back

the ghosts of native brothers and sisters of this tropical climate seers

grade school, high school never told of their existence

Indian land was far away in another world, across states lines where
    grandparents plant corn and herd sheep on a brown-eyed/blue-
    eyed horse . . .

I always forget L.A. has sacred mountains.

Jenny Holzer Inspiration

Circles
linking people in a room
as same
but
when we leave
I will remember
White _____
makes me nervous

          quiet
          + shut up

I will act
Indian
makes me nervous

          quiet
          + shut up

On Relocation

The physical is easier to achieve
a boundary drawn to separate people
Navajos say no word exists
establishing form to the air we breathe.

This country's stem
relocation
rooted for invasion
imperial in destiny.

WORKING, MEN
IN PROGRESS

Stand and wait for crossblood babies
generic cultures blending new versions of red nations
brain-dead at birth from pollution ingested
umbilical cord of sweet grain alcohol and sticky TV diaries.

WHO IS TO SAY?
crossblood babies
relocated at birth.

Check One:

        ☐ Diné
        ☐ Other

Bringing Hannah Home

We brought Hannah home today
in afternoon sun with a crisp chill in the air
on a hill overlooking the bay.

Two women with a child and a shovel and a frozen placenta wrapped
   in aluminum foil placed in a red plastic bag.
Hannah was brought into this world
some say fourth others say fifth
five days before.
Before we brought her home.

The weekend of rain softened the earth
but the cold discouraged the shovel from denting more than the
   surface.
I dug into the earth.
The ground weakened beneath the strength I put into the shovel
pounding the ground
smooth and moist at first
then cold and solid.

Pounding the ground
warmed my arms.
I thought good thoughts for Hannah and her mother
and prayed for us all.
Remembering those who have passed on and those to be born
and I thought of my children to be born
and I thought of my father who has passed on.

Breaking into the cold ground
I thought of the day we brought my father home.

Dinétah winter had frozen the ground
and the earth chipped like ice, slivers of crunchy cold beneath our
    feet.
Our bodies warmed by our work
and the earth chipped like an old tree being chopped, taking hours to
    finish.
Our bodies tired from our work
and the earth piled high beside the hole like the clouds and just as
    fluffy.
Our bodies natural returning to the ground.

I dug into the ground
digging out earth that would nourish Hannah
digging out life that would embody Hannah
and soon a small hole appeared four feet deep.

There we stood
two women with a child and a shovel and a frozen placenta wrapped
    in aluminum foil placed in a red plastic bag.
The frozen mass of
tissue and blood and life
was placed in the small hole
by Hannah's mother
and I felt her heat
tissue and blood and life
squatting with bloodied hands and cold earth
bringing Hannah home.

March 11, 1995

It was the year after Tázhii was born
a double rainbow greeted us home.
The next day
the clouds spread in swirls over the sky.
My hands touched cold mutton
feeling for the precise area on the joint
to cut
hack away at
with a saw
then toss it on the pile of meat
in the baker-size tin bowl.

I was told not to wash for four days
on the third day
I washed the grit of road travel off.

The circle of family united
to refasten the knot
with shiny brown faces of new children
a feast to warm tummies from chilly spring wind
joke-talking about what we'd really be doing if we had it together.
As people trailed away
the knot tightened and each gathered in her own way
to settle the stomach.

I saved the sheep head for my husband.
Wool charred from the fire pit
ears still soft and teeth still white
cooked just right
the perfect delicacy.

Ruthie Rae, My Kid

I first knew you in the womb
echoing my heartbeat
twisting your life cord
churning Thai green curry #17.

Now you smile at sunrise
praying in your language to our creator
tiny palms reach upward
fingers tracing
circles
like the spirals on your skull.

Your parents stumble like yourself
reaching for objects.

Your world
honey dips my Indian tea.

I pollute you with my thoughts
lest you starve
I am trapped by your hunger.

My little image
displaying my bad habits.

Case Study #311,990

I.
Many times
I exist in a form
acknowledged
without definition.
Is there a form
posing to exist
as a reverse?
Absence of being?
My response to linear expression
places me
tangent
to other objects of place.
My existence
tarnished from recognition.
A scorn of ignorance
complemented with its absence
struggles against
the space
with no apologies
and absolute forms.

II.
If I were Chinese
I could exist
as Meimei.
But I am Diné
known according to

English language.
In Diné bizaad
Asdz'aan Tłógí nishlí
Dezbah dóó atsóí yázhí bímá.
The passageway to my existence
is my tongue.
I take the role of little sister.
I take the role of Zia woman
and mother.

Indian Mom

for Faye

She cuts beading thread with her teeth
Her baby feeds from Similac breasts and Mickey D's cheeseburgers
I met her trading dreamcatcher earrings for blues CDs
I told her I was looking for a smoked hide
and we hit the road north to Crow Fair.

From a nomadic tribe of the northern plains
her home is where her children are
including her old man.
She spoon-feeds oatmeal.

I ain't ever seen her cry
so I figure
her tears are stitched into her beadwork
tight in rows
mending her own hoop.

Euro-American Womanhood Ceremony

Some say the boarding school experience wasn't that bad
because they learned a trade
at least the men did

The women
they were trained to specialize in domestic household work
to mimic the rituals of Euro-American women
to cook roast beef and not mutton
to eat white bread and not frybread
to start a family and not an education
to be happy servants to doctors' families in Sierra Madre
and then to their own

The young women who never really became women because they
    were taken off the rez before they could go through a womanhood
    ceremony
the young women who adapted to the Euro-American version of a
    womanhood ceremony

Instead of fasting and sweating and praying and running
They set the table and vacuumed and ironed and nursed and fed
and gave birth and birth and birth to a new nation of mixedbloods
and urban Indians
And they were mothers/providers/wives
They were strong and loved and made love and sobered up
and organized weekend road trips back to the rez
Back to the rez where we all came from
and where we need to return
to heal our wounds
from the Euro-American womanhood ceremony.

Asdz'aan Tó'dichi'níí

She was dad's baby sister
horsetail hair
swished across her butt

She had Nálí's image
bold
nose with roomy nostrils
to twitch when she disapproved
cheekbones were full moons
her big teeth glowed against her brown skin

She drove her Dodge Dart across the Little Colorado River
when dad's city truck spun its wheels
she waved bye with a beer can and two honks

She told me once why she married that bilagáana from the military
"He bought me beer," she said
"He never complained
The best part was changing my name
I thought his name would take my battered-old heart away
but it just got worse
I guess the easiest heart to love is your own."

That was the year she split from him
the summer was dusty
soft from cool evening sunsets
Her visit home was permanent

One afternoon
she slaughtered four rabbits
all I saw was the bloody wood stump

Later
after we gnawed on rabbit bones
she handed me a lucky rabbit foot
dried blood stained the white fur brown
the fresh rabbit foot in my pocket attracted lots of dogs
so I moved it to my jewelry box

When she finally had kids
they were from her second husband
His murder in town ended their vows
so she left her kids and moved to Phoenix

She visioned her death a year before
So she began giving her worldly items away
so her grave would be roomy
not cluttered with the trinkets that catalogued
her life of combing the sediment on the bottom of the river
She was dad's baby sister
Her head touched dad's chin when they hugged good thoughts
and by and by
and bye and bye

II.

This is from the center of
my skull where all is cosmic
and glacier washed from
reading journals of cultural
research called *Paris Review*
and *onthebus*. From the
melodic muse in my belly I
create what lives: survival
of colored peoples in this
country called the United
States. The cosmos, meteor-
showered with oppression,
cramps my back and balls
my fists, smashing the glass
ceiling against my nose,
bony and intricate are these
stories.
From Ruby she wails . . .

Ruby Awakens

Red
I find myself
sitting on a hard bench
doing quillwork
quillwork I can't believe
on a pair of jeans

What the fuck
this is useless
fuckin' A
dusty travelers pounding my head with sharp tack stares
bus terminal bench laughing so loud
I can't hear the time

I find myself
without memory
doing star quillwork
sitting on my bare ass
'cause the jeans are mine

What the fuck are you looking at
fuckin' A, I hate white people
a tall gothic clock with crossed eyes won't give me the time
chiming out of spite

Red
with no memory
I slip on my jeans
star quillwork on my ass
cold marble floor with faces

gnaws my bare feet
Where's the bathroom?
I ask the gothic clock and the marble floor
and I can't hear them 'cause the travelers start pounding the tacks with
    their feet
I fuckin' hate white people

The bus terminal bathroom
fun house
with two dingy-green rows of stalls
and I can't find my way to the toilet
so I squat to pee
and the mirror in front of me
starts crawling like a panther
and the sink flash floods

What the fuck
fuckin' A, what happened
streaked red
bloodied red
I'm bruised red with swollen cheek
squatting
staring into the shiny ceramic tiled floor
looking for my memory.

Ruby's Summer Fruit

I walk down the street
red with happiness
glowy as summer fruit
carrying a brown bag
peaches, nectarines, pears and grapefruit

Walking red
curvy down the street
arms full of fruit
headed home
three-story apartment building
off Fruitvale Avenue near MacArthur Boulevard

Walking into beauty
beauty with dark hair
smiling with the morning
and me ripe with summer fruit
drop my bag
as sex gushes off my body
down the street after beauty

Ruby Roast

Snapping grease
sizzling flesh
on L.A. streets

Over the years
slow baking
at 250 degrees

Red turning smog yellow-brown
haze ugly-deep

Yellow-brown tender
bloody-rare
obstructs the heart
blinds the eyes
vision of confusion
tunneling digestion
through skin

Urban Indian
already eaten

Ruby in the Sky

Empty Bud cans pushing McDonald's bags out the door
somewhere in New Mexico
arms stretching high
cold sky
space
frosting my hands
glowy as stars
twilight dipping me
merry-go-round
home
full-moon
belly-achin'
birthing

Magic dust showers
massages into hot springs bath
picture of Jesus Christ hanging above the front door
alcohol reassuring my action
carousel horses by my side
jeweled milky way
angelic bright
dripping stars from white manes

How Ruby Saves Laughter
for Les

I have a Ponca friend named Sailor
with a sweet windy voice that brushes away dirt and grime
you will know when you meet him
probably at the Hilltop on a Sunday after
you thought you'd never laugh
the sour stench from your stomach
out of your skull

Poncas got this magic
maybe it's the Oklahoma easy way of things
but Sailor sure sweeps me clean of dust
Whenever I see Sailor
I tell him
Take care of yo' skull, Sailor
'cause
Poncas
you see
are hard to find
so I say one more time
to my friend of three years
Sailor
you be careful
'cause
you see
Sailor is a Gentle Man
doin' time for the wrong reasons
so before I kiss his cheek *so long*

I give him a coffee can
tellin' him
Sailor
bein' an Indian's rough
bein' a Ponca's tougher
'cause
ain't hardly any around
so
when you get bruised and bloody again
you betta' collect your blood in this can
'cause
yo' blood's hard to come by
and more people need to laugh.

Disco Danny AKA Ruby's Dance Partner
for DJE

Oh *please*
don't tell me disco started
with Saturday Night Fever
no, no, no
the White Mountain Apache have the disco moves
way before John T.
crown dancers
sweet talk of hips
under moon-spotlight
Disco Danny
in denial
tease of
dancing crown
dangling charms
earth dance floor
tease reversal
stripping off Western
naked at birth
decorated
with honors
prance of deer
shake of cottontail thumping
waking the lazy
muscle of bridled horse
weighted by the human brain.

Ruby at Bat

Ruby plays softball
in desert sun
with SPF 15

Her legs forget how to deer sprint
so she rubs Icy Hot on her limbs to remember

The bat she pounds the ball with
feels good in her hands
solid and light
like her strength
a few years ago

She chooses to love the dusty kids
running to every relation for sno-cone money
a fifty-cent smile rimmed with strawberry juice

She sits on a tailgate and sells her aunt's burritos and pop
makes her own money
raffling a case of Coors
on Sunday

Her grandpa makes it to every tournament
seated behind the backstop
wearing cowboy hat and long-sleeve plaid shirt
basking in ninety-degree sun
watching over his grandchildren.

Ruby Stew

At the grave with no tears
memory bone dry

Four-year brew
thaw
flesh sensitive
simmer on shoulders

Sheep fat skims edge
pot of mutton stew
swirling formless form
on top of the greater entity

Where's my ladle?
spreading film like water
beneath
sweet onions
celery
potatoes soft on the tongue

Red in stew
of my father's death.

How Art Opens Ruby's Eye

Art Gallery Opening
Berkeley, California 1992

Invited to see art through native
hands more than image
of you drunk
-en
greasy _____
No longer from buffalo
capitalist grime
is slick to worn-down soles.

The White-filled gallery
does not know
I feel their grime
the backwash
left in clear plastic wine cups
the backwash
I swallow
as my brother sells his art.

Ruby's Bird Cage

Backroads driveabout
dusky rivers three embrace
over an island of green bog
invite us to
stop and pee
out the few dollars and change
we spent on beer.
Spring green tickles my ass
cool air from mating geese holding hands
dries it.

Nearby honks lead tiny feather puffs across the lake
Ruby honks back
and there is silence
same silence as bar talk
Whites who hear us chirp
buy us beer to keep our mouths shut.

Ruby Hikes

I.
Rests belly
on a bed rock
belly against stone
nurses

II.
Third World belly
on the woman hill
protruding
round
eternal with life

III.
Lying on my back
there is sex on this rock
whispering to my hands
sending sparkles to my bones
flashing red passed
of my

    ☐   collection
    ☐   memory
    ☐   heart
    ☐   back pocket

IV.
I wake up wet on the rock
soaking in the puddles
of my

- ☐ collection
- ☐ memory
- ☐ heart
- ☐ back pocket

Ruby in Me #1

middle child
smart child
¼ Navajo
                    ¼ Navajo
                        ¼ Navajo
                                ¼ Navajo

four parts equal my whole
#311,990

enrolled = proof
50
80
100 if you can stand
it

veiled
minority status
alcohol
resemblance

Ruby in Me #2

From the marrow in my bones
sometimes sucking it dry
tapping mother's milk

Then re-supplying
injecting words found along the spine of my structure
to re-
member from my own vessel
my way home
re-
living words prickly
re-
locating out of my mouth in spit

Like petting a cat
Ruby meows

Ruby's Answer

Sunny day, Southern California restaurant, February 11, 1990. While eating lunch, Ruby is confronted by a blonde woman with frosted hair and gold wire-rimmed Ray-Bans. The woman claims sisterhood with Ruby saying, "I know exactly how you feel because I'm part Indian myself." This is Ruby's response:

If you're Indian
I'm a WASP
White Indians aren't Indians, blondie
Indians survive
You mixed and assimilated and trashed and denied your Indian
blood
You want to claim and regain your Indian identity . . .
maybe in another life
Why all of a sudden do you want to be Indian?
Why do you want to be considered a minority?
An insignificant, inferior piece of red trash?
Why do you want to go from historically supreme to historically
oppressed?
Why do you want to be a statistic and a census number and a
dropout and a drunk and a savage and a squaw or a princess and a
car and a mascot and completely exploited until you no longer want
to be Indian?
Are you on crack or did you just get a vision from your great-
great-great-Cherokee grandma?
Blondie, this isn't the Girl Scouts
This is religious freedom and unrecognition and Big Mountain and
releasing brother Leonard Peltier

Indians don't "come out" like gay people
They are wiped out by the people that gave you most of your
blood!

Ruby didn't mind getting kicked out of the restaurant because she got
  a free lunch.

Ruby's Welfare

Standing in line
after being told
Indians don't stand in line
'cause a Kiowa woman at window #6
helps the skins

Time passes me
still in line

Man at window #1
tells me welfare is a luxury
and how come I don't have a job
check the time
I smile
place my forms in the box marked
LEAVE FORMS HERE
black black and bold
welfare is a luxury
place your form in our box
play by our rules

I laugh
sit
smoke a Virginia Slim
and talk to the spirits

People talk about luxury
but what they mean is obligation
to remain lower class

for food
$5.15 an hour
doesn't feed three

Again
I check the time
light another Virginia Slim
not finished with the spirits

Luxury
the U.S. forgot the definition
forgetting who allowed them to create the U.S.
obligation of treaty
honored through
IHS and a truckload of commods
luxury overextended
obligation 500 years behind

Ready to light Virginia Slim #3
I'm called by window #6

Ruby and Child

Memory is tricky
going deep into your bones
calcium sweet with nourishment
as mutton ribs on tongue
chewy in mouth
greasy like frybread.

Memory will kick in like last year's acid trip
when the earth sang out like the Black Lodge Singers
grand entry
calling all nations to dance
and your feet will know the song.

Memory is intricate
weaving charms of beauty way
bundles of wool
sheared from sheep
dyed with roots
like old-growth trees
recording time.

Falling Stars

With Ruby at my side
I hitchhike in moonless night
twelve-pack in my jacket
cans cold
weigh down my sleeves
clink clink
chilling my tits

We left the truck
cause it wasn't ours
but we bought the beer

No more swallowing the carbonated
cold years erased with the smash
of a can and the pop open of another
another pop open of the hips releasing one
more statistic smashing head open the glass ceiling
sealing us
vacuum-packed
neat into cases

The moon becomes our destination
as Ruby and I walk black tar uphill
climbing a horizon of pitch
taking our place with the stars in the sky

III.

My step is *crisp, crisp* when I
    need a *crunch, crunch*.
My heat is warm and soft,
    tucked away in the folds
    of history.
My story, flesh over tissue
    and blood, bulging with
    fatty promises.
My physical is no longer
    appealing the way I
    remember.
My memory poses to be
    discriminated against
    walls of unconscionable
    activity.
My climbing machine is no
    longer extending my
    horizon . . . and I do wish
    for locomotion among
    the whirlpool of unrecog-
    nizable.

Dry Spell

It's like the time
feeling really
playing with the real
like you really know
diamonds are beautiful even if you don't own one.

To Imagine Her Whole, Once More
for Karen

And she hides behind her dark wavy hair.
Allows it to grow for protection
mask her scars'
presence.
She entered this world
and she did not choose her existence
but she did choose a veil of dark wavy hair.
Limited choices
leading her
imagining her back home
providing her with dark wavy hair
for protection.

I heard her story once sipping beers at Larry Blake's
the blues band screamed out her story so she just smiled
And I smiling too
admiring her shawl of protection.

949 Agua Fria

O Today I see the way it is
The video repairman works earnestly for a corrupt boss
The next-door neighbor wakes at four in the morn to sell papers on
   the corner of Alicia and Hickox
The sun rises in a city where a handful pray on bended knee
The nation of natives gamble their land to Ernest and Julio Gallo in
   disposable Dixie cups
The planet's topsoil is fertile with multicultural vegetables
The waiter juggles six tables, the woman at table 35 wears no bras-
   siere, the plate rings when it drops
The mother slams the door, the child's tears scream the scars
And so I wake in my land of enchantment.

Sending the Letter Never Sent

> . . . all I can do is moan.
> And yet, if I didn't tell you,
> I would be angry at you for not listening,
> blaming you for what I haven't spoken.
> —David Mura

And wail
my anger trapped in my own brain cells
the thought behind the unspoken
is more than
what rolls off the tongue

From
those whose tongue is only in the first ceremony
the many ceremonies to follow
voice the unspoken

And those who speak
get plump from decorated shells of modernism

My own shame catches
as my brain shouts at itself
voice cracked and sore

You will not

Listen, I know I told you it before
yeah, yeah, Indians have their land stolen
yeah, yeah, it sucks we use them as mascots
yeah, yeah, tell me something new

I want to know why
skins drink so much
call themselves Indians

There's no real reason to complain
we're still around
breeds mostly
blending cultures generic
proud to be made in America
living off the fruits of its land
BIA
CIA
USA

Just say no
Just say it's a long story
my mind is telling
not for just one sitting
hundreds of winter evenings
to tell all these stories
No instant just add water
this is telepathic

Long ago
we believed the same
and difference only made our faith stronger.

For Miss Celine When She Smokes

Miss Celine is bold
and brown
and beautiful
and Damn
I cannot believe she is only 21

And man, can she guzzle beer
and smoke cigarettes
one by one
one after the other

And all the time while she smokes
I am thinking
I hope she is thinking good thoughts
because the spirits are listening

And I believe they listen to us while we talk
and I keep telling Miss Celine this
because she talks a lot while she smokes
one cigarette after another

As she fires up
Miss Celine is signaling the spirits to gather around
As she inhales
they are waiting for her to speak
As she exhales
they hear her words and listen
and they are sitting all around her
chatting about her and with her
Her advisors in a cloud of smoke

And through the tobacco
she talks with them
And through her smoke
they listen

But I know Miss Celine forgets about the spirits
so I try to think good thoughts for her.

Night Travel

I.

I like to travel to L.A. by myself
My trips to the crowded smoggy polluted by brown
indigenous and immigrant haze are healing.
I travel from one pollution to another.
Being urban I return to where I came from
My mother
survives in L.A.
Now for over forty years.

I drive to L.A. in the darkness of the day
on the road before CHP
one with the dark
driving my black truck
invisible on my journey home.

The dark roads take me back to my childhood
riding in the camper of daddy's truck headed home.
My brother, sister and I would be put to sleep in the camper
and sometime in the darkness of the day
daddy would climb into the cab with mom carrying a thermos full of
    coffee and some Pendleton blankets
And they would pray
before daddy started the truck
for journey mercies.

Often I'd rise from my lullaby sleep and stare into the darkness of the
    road
the long darkness empty of cars

Glowy from daddy's headlights and lonesome from Hank Williams'
    deep and twangy voice singing of cold nights and cheatin' hearts.

About an hour from Flagstaff
the sun would greet us
and the harsh light would break the darkness
and we'd be hungry from travel and for being almost home.

II.
I know the darkness of the roads
endless into the glowy path before me
lit by the moon high above and the heat rising from my truck's
    engine.
The humming from tires whisper mile after mile
endless alongside roadside of fields shadowy from glow.

I know the darkness of the roads
It swims through my veins
dark like my skin
and silenced like a battered wife.
I know the darkness of the roads
It floods my liver
pollutes my breath
yet I still witness the white dawning.

2 + 2 = Too Much

I.
Twice in the last two days
I drive a different man home
sleepy
exhausted from the energy put into a man

II.
Amused by his handsome smooth face
talk to him with my eyes
smiling pretty at me from across the table
me smiling pretty back when he pours beer into my glass
smiling pretty still
feeling the lazy of the beer
Mr. Pillow Talk
I wanna fall asleep right on your chest
Mr. Pillow Talk just keeps smiling pretty at me from across the table
Mr. Pillow Talk with nice hands
lean fingers caressing his beer glass
bringing it to his lips
smiling pretty
his face pretty and smooth
I wanna touch it
cup it with my hand and touch the prettiness
let him drink my touch
My touch too hard spills beer
Mr. Pillow Talk with nice hands gets a rag from the bar
Mr. Pillow Talk with nice hands also has a nice ass
Nice ass

Nice smile
Nice night.

III.
The second man
shows age on his face
smiling in ways I remember
with dancing eyes boyish dewy-new
Smiling in ways to make me care
with grin well-deep
and we talk
eyes first
scanning the years
then nothing
'cause memory won't let me go any further
Holding each other
the heat once there
is now lost
in the well of his grin.

"49" in a Mountain Town

Indian bars
all ages
can meet.

Indian bars.
Rather unites all
into colonial vestiges.

Indian bars
smoky hues
spindled of urban
of hyperamerica
greasy-to-the-last-drop grime
conditioned by the invasion.
If conversion
then reversion.
We will know as a twister.

"49" in a mountain town.
Biting chill of spring
sobers all
eventually.

On Telly Biliizh

Most skins drink it drank it at least once
reaction to our mouths pinned shut when The Thumb Print was
        stamped into parchment and when cousin Deena says, "Let's
        get *sauced* up!"
Twisting that cap to slurp down some of that radioactive liver-eating
        spirited shit
is us/skins/me/you

Indoctrination more lethal than any missionary
gurgling bubbles in your ear like a one-night snag
it coughs up bits of memory that seep into the earth
Our mother cleansing us one more time
She holds our truth
spit no longer digestible until
your body writhes for more like that skin at Indian Alley with mucus
        shined face saying, *Hey, little sister, can you spare some* . . .

and you wanna say *Fuck off and get outta the gutter*
but you're too chicken to say what's on your mind so you continue . . .
Indoctrination worse than government
'cause you kill him with that dollar
might as well smash his head into that stone wall he's leaning against
Hell, he already done half the job for you
won't ever know what happened
probably most pleased to be released from the brick-wall sanctuary

So just do it

When Roots Are Exposed

I.
The empty of stomach
manifests silence
a stillness
that levels
coffee in a cup
and in a respectful manner
allows steam to penetrate
the surface.
Reversal of action
has created my sandstone canyon
rooted cedar and sage at my feet.
This movement is where
a tranquility stems.

II.
When my child creates
bubbles through a soapy wand,
I occupy the action of fate
that bursts the perfect form.
A halcyon absorbed
nesting within
the existence of the form
that no longer exists.
The formless form
is where my mind floats.

III.
It is easy to give form
especially with English words

a promotion of mechanical ligaments
binding spirit with assembly-fabricated molds.
Just as my hair poses an appendage of my brain
my tongue poses an appendage of my heart.
I cannot classify this thought as a typewritten symbol.
An ideogram of essence
cultivates my stillness to action.

To the Word "Indian"

Native struggle is worried and its back broke
bending at the waist like a
Social Security recipient and a Las Vegas whore

Slow assassination

IV.

This essay churned in my belly until it finally rose out of my limbs and gave itself form. It has been previously shared.

In the Cycle of the Whirl

RE-ENTRY

My mother is my story.

She sacrificed for me, allowing me to use the enemy's tongue.
Perhaps to reverse the process. Perhaps to change the process.
Perhaps so I could survive the process easier than she.

To acknowledge that I can manipulate the English language is to tell my her-story or re-tell shimá.

To acknowledge that I can manipulate the English language is to
say my tribal language is scrambled within me. In my blood silently
circulating. In my back pocket squashed incomprehensible. The color
of my skin. The rhythm, ba-bum, the ticking, ba-bum, the map in my
heart, ba-bum, leading me home.

My path predetermined by my blood?

That is the Diné will and spirit. And I am thankful I inherited this
beauty.

FIRST LIGHT

In the beginning, there was darkness. But by the time we emerged to
the Fourth World, many things existed. Especially grandmothers.
Shinálí said prayer is part of our survival, giving thanks, manifesting
our destiny. Many of the things given to us contribute to our sur-
vival—not because we deserve it, but because our creator planned it.

I only remember listening to the nasal low and high tones sounding
like a chanter speaking powerful words. I would see the words flow
over my body, tingling my skin. My recollections come from the
instructions I received as a child. Instructions in the husky syllables of
the Navajo language. Instructions familiar and natural.

Don't kill spiders because they are your grandmothers. Don't kill horned toads because they are your grandfathers. Rub one on your chest for good luck. Talk to your relatives and learn from their habits. Never be afraid of them. Never refuse food offered to you, especially if it's mutton. When you butcher a sheep, eat all the parts or use them to make rugs or clothing.

Know your clan. Know your language because someday only Indians who know their language will be recognized. Learn the ways of the bilagáana but don't forget where you came from. To avoid bad luck, burn the hair that's tangled in your brush. Help shimá with the frybread. Wave your arms over the fire and talk to it. Be careful of who you shake hands with when your parents aren't with you. There are werewolves about. Hogans are open in the east to greet the sun.

Don't sleep late or the sun will strike you dead.

FACTS

Born July 2, 1968, in Gallup, New Mexico, in the old Indian Hospital on the hill. Raised urban among Los Angeles skyscrapers, Mexican gangs, Vietnamese refugees, eating frybread and beans. Middle child. Father from Birdsprings. Mother from Torreon. Daughter of Eddie and Susan. U.S. Federal Indian Relocation Policy placed them into boarding schools away from the rez. Five-Year Program at Sherman Institute, Riverside, California. Goal: annihilation of savage tendencies characteristic of indigenous peoples. New language. New clothes. New food. New identity. Learn to use a washing machine. Learn to silence your native tongue, voice, being. Learn to use condiments without getting sick. Learn a trade and domestic servitude. Learn new ways to survive.

Whisper in Navajo after the lights go out. Rise early to pray.

Eddie and Susan, married 1963. Three children. Decided not to teach us the Navajo language. Two to three months out of every year was spent on the Navajo Reservation. Definition: place where the sun toasts your skin with color from its painted desert after spring showers and the oozing silence thunders with your heartbeat. Close family. Always close(d). Fall 1982, freshman in high school. Shinálí died.

Went back to Birdsprings for two weeks. Anger. Anger for death. Anger for going back. Didn't go to burial. Piercing blade of random anger. 1985, daddy started getting sick and his granddaughter, Alexandria, was born. Then daddy's grandma died. 1986, graduated from Earl Warren High School. UCLA or UC Berkeley? UC Berkeley. Daddy died on Wednesday, October 14, 1987. Withdrew for a year.

Anger. Anger from my sour heart. Anger at him for leaving us. Hard on mom. Anger for his silence. Anger for giving me his dreams and desires. Transferring *victim* to me. My inheritance. Confusion. Changes too fast. Native lifestyle scrambled in assimilationist's mixing bowl. New patriarchal ingredients = no time to heal. Recovery is relearning. Returned to school.

VOICE INSIDE

The amusement of the reservation never wore off because there was always good fun: herd sheep, jump arroyos, ride horses, play BB gun tag, card games. I never realized those happy times in my life would end, could end.

Returning to California from the rez, I always felt different. Some sort of transformation occurred on the rez, like visiting a mystery land. Spacious, almost no boundaries, I was free to roam, unlimited, freed from streetlights and cars and territorial gang warfare. The only limitation was mother natural, and somehow I seemed to break all her rules. I was constantly told not to touch this or capture that creature. I was unaccustomed to the mutual respect between people, the land and animals.

The two worlds often clashed in me, creating blackness, a voice yearning to shout with boldness, the way my aunt uses the Navajo language to get after grandkids or tell a joke.

The rez has changed as I've grown older. Grandparents, like our land's vast beauty, seemed eternal. Aged with spirit yet never old. Animate and lively, never dead. Those relations shape the path my feet travel, still, even after they've left this earth.

I look at *shicheii's* summer camp, trying to imagine shimá hauling water and herding sheep with my aunts and uncles. Two aunts and one uncle still live in Torreon. They are all educators, working for elementary day schools. They deal daily with the trickle-down bureaucracy the BIA passes on to Diné, further down to local chapters. The economy of domestic dependent nationhood dehumanizes, re-invents natives as chattels to be directed, displayed, and researched. As survivors of boarding school "education," a process of pure indoctrination and rigid transformation, their voices remain bottled.

The bottle containing the silenced voices hums. It hums old songs and whispers past lives. A sitting ghost, its coming unknown. Though I've seen the ghost, I can only ponder the lore it contains.

In the summer of 1993, I worked in Torreon teaching creative writing classes to young people through the Torreon Counseling Services. I was excited to have a job on the rez and the challenge of re-experiencing the place of mystery and good fun. Living there as a grown woman was worlds away from what I remembered as a child.

The population of our little corner of the rez was thriving. HUD housing communities had been built and more were in progress, creating some employment. However, most residents are not permanently employed. A small Thriftway trading store was still the closest source for groceries, gas, and video rentals. As a kid, the land was immense and magical. No matter how much skin and blood I left on mesas and in arroyos, I continued to explore its crevices. That has not changed. The majesty of the land comforts the chaos that seeps down.

The rez is another nation. Another worldview that functions in a space relevant only to the elements, strung together with language that also relies on the elements. The space is so specific, translation is impossible. My English voice and Western thoughts struggle with the small Navajo vocabulary in my head. TV and other media sources open a new dimension of crossblood simulation. Re-routing tribal identity with capitalist influences. Every little kid I worked with knew who Michael Jordan and Shaquille O'Neal are and how much money they made. Very few knew the name of our tribal president. In my generation and before, access to outside influences was not as disarming. Urban streethood appeals as much to rez kids as traditional ceremonies. Our nation competes with itself.

I took the responsibility to share my institutional knowledge with my classes. I exposed them to Third World writers, mostly women in the United States. My texts were the anthologies *Dancing on the Rim of the World* (edited by Andrea Lerner), *Haciendo Caras/Making Face, Making Soul* (edited by Gloria Anzaldúa), *This Bridge Called My Back* (edited by Gloria Anzaldúa and Cherríe Moraga), *That's What She Said* (edited by Reyna Green), and my own writings and videos. I confronted them with postcolonial thought from Trinh T. Minh-ha, bell hooks, and Gloria Anzaldúa. Key in translating Third World experience, these writers connect the dots to provide vivid descriptions of survival under colonial rule.

My students, as young writers, left me with the inspiration to continue writing and teaching. Since my position was not permanent, I was able to plant the seed of revolution but will never know how tall and strong the plant grows.

Sometimes I think the land has endured much better than my relatives. We have all gone different directions, and few of those directions have led to higher education. Three in my extended clan have completed bachelor's degree programs. Three lives have ended from alcohol abuse. Many more remain affected and clenched by the spirit of alcohol. In conflict with our creator, the spirit of alcohol feeds off wounds acquired from centuries of genocidal battle. In a state of colonial confusion, the rez calls out to me to recycle and be cleansed.

I used to let my deep brown skin tint my image second-class. My nose narrow with a slight arc like the stoic Indian seen on old-time nickels. My skin glowing with red tones reflecting cedar-covered mesas. I see my image, captured and bound in Edward Curtis photographs, carrying water jugs from contaminated rivers. Biological warfare. But our creator is stronger.

¼ + ¼ + ¼ + ¼ = FOUR PARTS = MY WHOLE

Who I am is determined by my mother. I am Tł'ógí, Zia clan, related to Tódich'íí'nii, Bitterwater clan. I am the granddaughter of Pearl Toledo and Richard Antone. My nation is matrilineal and distinguishes maternal relations from paternal. *Shináli* is used for both paternal grandparents, while *shimásání* is maternal grandmother, and *shicheii* is maternal grandfather.

I remember the fourteen or fifteen dogs grandpa acquired. The dogs were all sizes and all strays. When he took them in, they returned his kindness by guarding his dwelling and livestock. He had to kill only one for attacking sheep. I used to help feed the dogs the government-issued commodity instant potatoes. Grandpa rode a motorcycle to herd the sheep and had a blue-eyed/brown-eyed horse. Grandpa took us to his summer camp and told us stories about the painted desert's magic and the werewolf. He spoke English and talked in gentle and slow words. With the same voice, he would sing Navajo songs.

Shinálí raised chickens and rabbits. She kept the chickens in a three-tiered shed with a chicken-wire door. The rabbits lived in an abandoned station wagon. All the seats were taken out and the rabbits made their homes out of old clothes and cardboard thrown about. She taught me how to gather eggs and chase rabbits. Sometimes, shinálí would ask me to go into the cellar and get some commodity-can juice. The cellar was a mud-packed mound hollowed out into the earth. When I was little, I was scared to go into its dark and cool atmosphere. Shinálí stored commods and dried mutton inside. One year, a sheep head rotted in there and the stench of spoiled meat never left its depths. Ruthie Slick was shinálí's name. She was a small woman. Every visit, she would adorn me and my sister with jewelry. She used too much salt when she ate.

I still enjoy sitting behind shicheii's house, listening to the humming silence, storing the heat in my memory. The lazy heat melts your ears to the earth and soon the ants begin to talk. Early in the morning, the announcer of the Navajo radio station becomes part of my sleep, running free, jumping high over mesas, soaring with great birds of prey. Only the country tunes played between bulletins stumble my journey.

Shimásání and I started weaving a rug together when I was ten. I never saw it finished. I was only reminded of it from an old photo. In the photo, my hands are on the rug working and my head turns toward the camera. The camera is turned downward toward me and with my expressionless face, I'm searching for guidance. Sometimes when I step into the coolness of shicheii's clay-walled house, I'll gaze at the photo hanging in a collage with other grandchildren's pictures. The photo was taken the same year I ate cold sheep stomach with shimásání.

Mom said we had to fight to get Torreon to be considered part of the Navajo Nation. Torreon is considered the Checkerboard Area. Shicheii remembers when our land extended out close to Albuquerque. Shicheii used to trade frequently with the Spanish in border towns and other tribes in nearby villages, so now he speaks three languages: Navajo, Spanish and English. My grandparents don't have birth certificates, but they have roll numbers. So do I; I was put on the rolls two years after I was born. My maternal grandparents are slowly withering away. I try to capture them on videotape, like the federal government, creating 2-D images that sit on shelves collecting dust.

I would like to document shicheii's life. He has seen many changes in the land, the boundaries delineating our existence, some years good, some bad. He has survived boarding schools, U.S. military service, shifts in tribal and U.S. government. He still tends his sheep, though the flock is much smaller. He's still active in the community, catching the bus to weekly senior citizen lunches and functions. In summer, he follows softball tournaments to watch his children and grandchildren play in the sun. He takes his place as tribal elder and historian as he sips on pop.

U.R.I.s. (Urban-Raised Indians). We are city cousins. The ones who didn't know how to ride. Or jump arroyos. Sometimes it didn't matter if you were fullblood because they knew you weren't from the rez. I was raised on a mixture of traditional knowledge and urban life. I used to think everyone ate frybread and mutton. If you were Indian, you were Navajo. If you were Navajo, then both parents were Navajo. I had no conception of mixedbloods. I thought all grandmothers lived in a hogan and could catch a sheep and butcher it, no problem. I did not know being urban could be such a disability. A degree from UC Berkeley will never change the fact that I cannot understand my grandfather when he asks for more coffee.

My early childhood memories are sweet and are slowly coming back to guide my path. There are also other memories which I chose to forget long ago that are returning to guide my path. I don't speak Navajo. I feel it in my thoughts, flowing from my mind smooth as the wind. My enduring culture has absorbed me unknow- ingly while I was playing with giant ant hills or helping to clean out the internal organs of a sheep. More than blood, my soul.

74

FIRST BITE

The night before I graduated from the University of California at Berkeley in spring 1991, I finally realized the gift. Being chosen to represent my classmates at our commencement, I was responsible for telling our story at graduation.

Every time I tried to write, all I saw were faces, not words: shinálí at dusk, sitting, pushing up her wire-rimmed spectacles; my mother shuffling around in the gray hours of the day; me in the halls of UC Berkeley saying "sorry" with my body as I move out of the way to allow others to pass; my father sitting in his armchair where I massaged his shoulders. After dinner while watching the news, he'd massage his own feet. His body wearing thin from work.

So I wrote about him.

After my first year at Berkeley, he died, and I withdrew for a year. During that year off, I worked for the City of Manhattan Beach doing clerical work full-time. I was making money and spending it fast, never focusing on goals. I didn't think about school until I had been working there almost a year. My brain began to crave the challenge I had started at Berkeley.

I was readmitted the following year and began developing my writing career through the Ethnic Studies Department Third World Moving Images course taught by Loni Ding and Robert Kaputof. This class enabled me to voice my concerns through the moving image. Once given the opportunity to re-create images, to re-tell stories, I utilized that medium to produce five videos and help found the Women of Color Film and Videomakers' Collective. The creation of native productions is overdue, and the heart of good productions is the story. Someday, I will put my story to screen.

As I began to write, I thought, how can I show that my time at Berkeley was similar to my parents' experience in boarding school? The tension of skin color. People asking, what country did you flee?

What island did you come from? The gnawing glare from eyes of those who questioned my place in this country. Then, when people discovered I was native, I was either ultra-cool or overprivileged. They assumed I received money and kickbacks from the government. Many of my classmates had no concept of natives, especially those indigenous to California. With such huge cities as Los Angeles and San Francisco, many non-natives considered themselves native because of the few generations their families had resided in the state.

There was no native dorm or club when I arrived. There was no native student orientation like they had for Chicano, black and Asian students. I did not meet any native students until my second semester, in two of my Native American Studies classes. The Native American Studies Department was our Indian Center. That department was the contact with the surrounding Bay Area community and campus. Berkeley made it easy for me to be an activist because of its free-speech history and because there were few native people on campus and little native history in classes.

Out of a student body of 30,000, 250 had registered themselves as native. The small group of us that reformed the Inter-Tribal Student Council often wondered where the couple hundred other skins were. As we began to investigate the list of students claiming native ancestry, we encountered an alarming number of students who checked the box "American Indian" fraudulently, using the native minority status to get into the university. Some traced their "American Indian" blood back many generations and had no knowledge of tribe. Some South Asian students from India were mistakenly checking the box. My outrage guided me to begin voicing my concerns early in my career as a student.

In the spring of 1990, Third World students congregated in thought and body to raise and demand issues of diversity among the faculty and the student body. Although the native population was small, there was a push by other students of color to voice our needs.

This thrust to participate physically was difficult, let alone awakening a voice silenced for hundreds of years. My voice and the voices of other natives on campus were not simply our own. We speak the voices of our nations, our clan relations, our families. To tell or re-tell our story is not pleasant. And it is not short. It did not begin with the civil rights movement. It is not as simple as the word genocide. It is every voice collective. It is mixedblood, crossblood, fullblood, urban, rez, relocated, terminated, non-status, tribally enrolled, federally recognized, non–federally recognized, alcoholic, battered, uranium-infested.

Every time I was asked to speak, I didn't know where to begin. Every time I shed tears, re-awakening old wounds, in an almost-prayer of thanks for those sacrificed. I questioned my presence in that institution for higher learning. Was I learning weapons necessary for battle?

These emotions and questions rushed my being. I had no previous examples from my family about battles in higher education. I only knew injustices existed and affected my family. I knew my father and mother deserved more money from employment than they were earning. I knew we ate beans and frybread over and over because meat was expensive and eating out was a special occasion.

I knew our state of emergency is still valid.

That was what pushed me to the microphone. Every time I spoke, I knew I was more privileged than most natives. Given the chance to voice. Perhaps change. Given the opportunity to witness institutional indoctrination, to see the process; injustice spills over the walls of institutions, splashing unknown passersby. My privilege was only as valid as my voice. I could legitimate our existence and need to survive tribally and within institutions like UC Berkeley when my voice, my weapon, was prepared for battle.

The microphone that echoed across Sproul Plaza was true isolation. Standing before the hundreds gathered who were waiting and willing to hear the words out of my mouth. Flashes crossed my mind depicting our state of emergency, and I would be in some border town standing in line at a trading store, waiting. . . . Negotiating ourselves for cans of coffee and sacks of sugar and flour. I would approach the gathered crowd with only my life stories. Again wondering about my place in this student movement. How did I blend? How did I get talked into speaking?

Others would get up and talk about the movement and revolution and cite Third World leaders. I would be left out trying to think of a radical native leader who said something to affect my life. Then I thought again and laughed.

Of course I never fit in because the Diné philosophy and worldview were always considered radical compared to Western thought. Such a different means of approach and conclusions.

Thus my trouble with the movement. Many times I felt our goals collided. Many of the students, even the Third World ones, were middle class. But class was never discussed much, which led to many assumptions. To speak out was easy for those with no jobs and noontime classes. Most never acknowledged the privilege of not having to maintain a job. The luxury of our existence in that university depended on our ability to pay tuition.

I was constantly reminded of my privilege simply by traveling home. I was awarded grant money to read literature and analyze theories of Manifest Destiny while my mother still worked two jobs. The irony always silenced me.

That day at graduation, I began the way I was taught, introducing my clans in Navajo. Then, I acknowledged that my language skills are in a foreign language, English. To acknowledge the use of an oppressor's tongue is to manifest the changes. All of us native students were graduating from institutional warfare, fighting the dominant influences of intellect that presses realities of domestic dependency.

The university was pleased to have "minority" students as long as we remained the minority, silenced. The expansion of our minds in university facilities was explosive enough to curtail the movements we started to repatriate skeletal and ceremonial remains of native peoples and to increase faculty diversity campuswide. The university stalled about commenting on our demands, hoping the issues would be forgotten, shelved.

With the strength of native nations collectively, our resistance and humor, I graduated. Our stories, mutual, linked to bridge reinforcement. Our journeys, separate, unite to uprise.

FROM THE STENCH OF MY BELLY

Sometimes there are experiences too delicate to re-live through memory, which often happens when re-told by the constructed yet sinuous voice of nonfiction. Sometimes the whimsical yet sinuous voice of poetry will suffice.

this is me from me about me to those whose own story is mutual

STOP

i don't know when i realized the whole picture
i know now that whatever happens i have been given the strength
through our creator to handle

PAUSE

my story is here and now and hopefully will discontinue very soon

STOP

others noticed i was different before i noticed i was different
when i was younger all i was told to do was play hard and rise
    before the sun

i tried very hard to follow those instructions

Slow down and breathe easy

i learned these instructions before i learned to remember

from my memory
i know how to pray
learned how to love
am here from endurance

my story is unique to my condition

*FLASH: DO YOU REMEMBER THAT PICTURE OF YOU AND
YOUR BROTHER EDDIE JR., THE ONE WHERE YOU ARE
TYING HIS SHOES?*

surviving in this place called the united states
is possible

impossible
for those who take it seriously

"if i were japanese
i would be a nisei
i am second-generation
off-reservation

my mother comes from
the land of enchantment
now also
the land of poverty
drugs
illiteracy
and confusion

my mother
like many japanese during world war II
was relocated
off the rez
to a federally run
boarding school
in riverside, california, USA"

my mother resides
angelic
among yellow-brown haze
indigenous and immigrant smog in Los Angeles
skyscraping progress pushing her home

DO YOU REMEMBER IN THE DUSK OF SUMMERTIME HOW WE
   WOULD MOW THE LAWN WITH DADDY AND MOM WOULD
   MAKE POPCORN?

i'm sure when you were young
your history books told you all about indians
or
i'm sure when you were young
you saw indians on TV
YOU SAW ME ON TV:
indian princess
rotund squaw
blood-thirsty brave
stoic chief
ungrateful drunk

ONE DAY I WAS RUNNING, FELL, SCRAPED MY KNEE AND THE
   BLOOD WAS RED AND I PUSHED YOU DOWN AND YOUR
   BLOOD WAS RED

now
i'm sure when you were young
your fifth-grade teacher couldn't tell you why

men worked on cars and built airplanes and school buses
men drank beer and played pool
they had friends named Buffalo Joe and Harold Jim
they laughed a lot and yelled a lot
and called white men chicken shit
men stayed at bars all weekend and wore dark glasses and sat in the back at
    church
their shame silenced and their anger roared you into an arroyo safe from them
and you didn't want to be like them
or know anyone like them
or love anyone like them
again

MY FATHER WAS NOT ONLY A MAN BUT A HERO YOU WILL NEVER READ ABOUT IN HISTORY BOOKS

when i was young
i saw men as father

as a grown woman
i see my father
become me

sitting in a bar
silencing the war cry of my mothers corralled at bosque redondo
numbing the wound deep in my valley of cowboys and indians
recycling the memory of cold mountain fever

DO YOU REMEMBER THAT PICTURE OF DADDY WITH DARK GLASSES HOLDING UP HIS POOL TOURNAMENT TROPHIES?

it is believed that my father was born in the year 1938
his birthdate has been recorded as october 23 and january 18
he was the son of ruthie slick, the daughter of marie tsosie
he was raised on goat's milk straight from the udder

*DO YOU REMEMBER SHINÁLÍ? HOW SHE USED TOO MUCH
    SALT ON HER MEAT?*

my father was a southpaw
stocky brown man
who loved to laugh
the game of pool
was his passion
he played doubles single-handed
a small-time legend at two-way inn

*DO YOU REMEMBER THE SOUND OF DADDY'S TRUCK WHEN
    HE PULLED IN THE DRIVEWAY?*

his face cool
reading the table
figuring out his next shot
settin' up the next dude
the next white dude
to give back
every time someone shouted, "hey chief!"
every underpaid job
every can of commodity food

ONE DAY I REALIZED THERE IS NO PAIN IN KICKING ASS

yeah, i imagine him now
at every break
every combination

every clean shot of the winning eight-ball
i see him

yeah, my dad won
the game of survival
in a place some call the united states
in a country where memory slits your throat
he won

this is my story
starring the terminated mythic indian created
remaining very much here in the homeland
recovering

SO HURRY, EAT SOME BLUE CORN MUSH
  BEFORE YOU PUKE

HOMEWARD

In the fall of 1992, I enrolled at the Institute of American Indian
Arts (IAIA) in Santa Fe, New Mexico. Never before had I attended an
institution for higher learning where the majority student population
was comprised of natives. This unique community has provided me
with a safe house to re-cover, un-cover, and dis-cover.

Self, voice, and existence have all been nourished and battered. I
have trained with instructors dedicated to looming voices of new
writers. Their commitment has brought in a series of Visiting Guest
Writers, opening our small program to the "established" writing
communities. Within small student writing circles, I am challenged
and amazed.

I am in the cycle of the whirl. The circle to complete my journey.
A Long Walk, perhaps battling new giants. My path has been blessed

with rich stories: my heirloom. With each pit stop along my journey, my collection of stories grows. The haven for emerging writers at IAIA is an inspiring working model. From the center of its skull, IAIA houses a furnace of voices, scrambled with signs of recovery, gagging on oppressors' tongues, a hope chest treasured with stories. From here I write. This point of trauma, twisting from depths of emergenc(y); hear, perhaps, listen with keen ears; our rage will transform.

The landscape of my writing will always focus on our struggles, from my memory, what I witness in my blood coursing through my veins, and stories overheard in bar-talk. The will of my writing rises from shimá, as daily as her morning prayers in the gray hours. The hunger in my writing feeds from my journey homeward.

Acknowledgments

Grateful acknowledgment is made to the editors of the following anthologies in which these poems (or earlier versions of them) originally appeared:

Both Sides, ed. David Fields (IAIA Press, 1994): "Ruby at Bat," "Indian Mom," "Ruby's Answer," "Euro-American Womanhood Ceremony"

Home Is in the Blood, ed. Eddie Chucalate (IAIA Press, 1995): "Ruby's Bird Cage," "Ruby and Child," "Falling Stars," "Ruby Hikes," "How Ruby Saves Laughter," "On Relocation," "On *Telly Biliizh*," "To the Word *Indian*"

It's Not Quiet Anymore, ed. Heather Ahtone and Allison Hedge Coke (IAIA Press, 1992): "Bringing Hannah Home," "2 + 2 = Too Much," "Night Travel," "Ruby Awakens," "Ruby and Child," "Ruby's Summer Fruit," "Ruby's Welfare"

Moving the Image: Independent Asian Pacific American Media Arts, ed. Russell Leong (UCLA Asian American Studies Center, 1991): "surviving in this place called the united states" (quoted in "In the Cycle of the Whirl")

Neon Pow Wow: New Native American Voices of the Southwest, ed. Anna Lee Walters (Northland Publishing, 1993): "Blues-ing on the Brown Vibe," "Bringing Hannah Home"

Speaking for the Generations: Native Writers on Writing, ed. Simon Ortiz (University of Arizona Press, 1998): "In the Cycle of the Whirl"

The epigraph to the poem "Sending the Letter Never Sent" is from *After We Lost Our Way*, by David Mura (National Poetry Series, 1989).

About the Author

Esther G. Belin is a writer who was raised in Lynwood, California. She is among the myriad of indigenous peoples on the planet to survive in urbanized areas. She graduated from the University of California at Berkeley and the Institute of American Indian Arts in Santa Fe, New Mexico. Her first published work appeared in *Moving the Image: Independent Asian Pacific American Media Arts*. Other published works appear in these anthologies: *Both Sides, Home Is in the Blood, It's Not Quiet Anymore, Neon Pow Wow, Song of the Turtle,* and *Speaking for the Generations*. She has two daughters and currently resides in Durango, Colorado.